For the most wonderful Dad

From:

_____

Dear Dad,
This special book is just for you,
Because I'm forever grateful for all you do.

With your words of encouragement, I stand tall,
You inspire me to give it my all.

You're my hero, brave and bold,
With a heart of purest gold.

You're my anchor in every storm,
In your arms, I'm safe and warm.

You take me on adventures near and far,
And show me how to wish upon a star.

You listen to my dreams and fears,
And always wipe away my tears.

I cherish the moments we spend together,
Your presence makes life even better.

From teaching me how to ride a bike,
To soaring kites and magical hikes.

You're the compass in my life's quest,
With your guidance, I am truly blessed.

When I'm feeling sad or down and blue,
You're the one who knows just what to do.

I love the way you tuck me in at night
And tell me stories 'til I sleep tight.

I cherish moments, big and small,
You're the greatest dad of all.

Your laughter fills the air with cheer.
Your smile and hugs ease every fear.

Through ups and downs, you're always there,
A constant source of love and care.

Your faith in me is steady and strong,
Your belief in me helps me carry on.

You've taught me values, respect, and grace,
In your footsteps, Dad, I find my place.

Thank you, Dad, for all that you do,
I'm forever grateful, and I love you.
Love,
Your little one

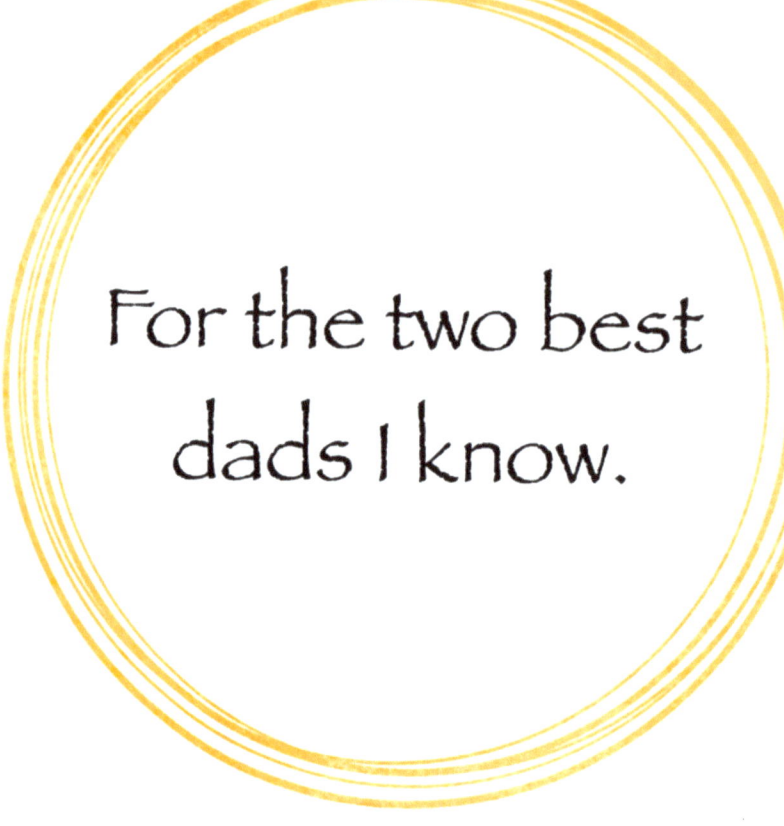

For the two best
dads I know.

Discover more
great books

https://www.llgray.com

www.ingramcontent.com/pod-product-compliance
Lightning Source LLC
Chambersburg PA
CBHW041459120626
46547CB00003B/481